HIDING HIPPOS: COUNTING FROM 1 TO 10

by Amanda Doering Tourville

illustrated by Sharon Holm

Content Consultant: Paula J. Maida, PhD, and Terry Sinko, Instructional Support Teacher

magic wagon

Published by Magic Wagon, a division of the ABDO Publishing Group, 8000 West 78th Street, Edina, Minnesota 55439. Copyright © 2009 by Abdo Consulting Group, Inc. International copyrights reserved in all countries. All rights reserved. No part of this book may be reproduced in any form without written permission from the publisher.

Looking Glass Library™ is a trademark and logo of Magic Wagon.

Printed in the United States.

Text by Amanda Doering Tourville
Illustrations by Sharon Holm
Edited by Patricia Stockland
Interior layout and design by Becky Daum
Cover design by Becky Daum

Library of Congress Cataloging-in-Publication Data

Tourville, Amanda Doering, 1980–

  Hiding hippos : counting from 1 to 10 / by Amanda Doering Tourville ; illustrated by Sharon Holm.

    p. cm. — (Count the critters)

  ISBN 978-1-60270-263-9

  1. Counting — Juvenile literature. I. Holm, Sharon Lane, ill. II. Title.

  QA113.T685 2009

  513.2'11 — dc22

           2008001608

Counting is fun! Count to ten as these hiding hippos surface from their watery homes to explore the world around them.

Hippos like to stay cool in the water. One hippo sprays water from its nose as it surfaces. Count it: one.

7   8   9   10   0+1=**1**

Hippos live together in African rivers. Two hippos slowly rise from the muddy water. Count them: one, two.

Hippos live together in African rivers. Three hippos gallop gracefully along the river bottom. Count them: one, two, three.

1 2 3 4 5 6

7 8 9 10 2+1=3

1 2 3 4 5 6

Hippos live together in African rivers.
Four hippos swish their tails back
and forth, marking their territory.
Count them: one, two, three, four.

Hippos live together in African rivers. Five hippos have stepped up on land to graze on grass. Count them: one, two, three, four, five.

7 8 9 10 4+1=5

1 2 3 4 5 6

Hippos live together in African rivers. Six hippos stand still while birds clean their skin. Count them: one, two, three, four, five, six.

Hippos live together in African rivers. Seven hippos call to the others with a grunt. Count them: one, two, three, four, five, six, seven.

1   2   3   4   5   6

7 8 9 10 6 + 1 = 7

Hippos live together in African rivers.
Eight hippos yawn, showing their
enormous tusks.

1 2 3 4 5 6

Count them: one, two, three,
four, five, six, seven, eight.

7 8 9 10 7+1=8

Hippos live together in African rivers. Nine hippos twitch their ears to shake water from them. Count them: one, two, three, four, five, six, seven, eight, nine.

1 2 3 4 5 6

7 8 **9** 10 **8 + 1 = 9**

Hippos live together in African rivers. Ten newborn hippos take their first breaths. Count them: one, two, three, four, five, six, seven, eight, nine, ten.

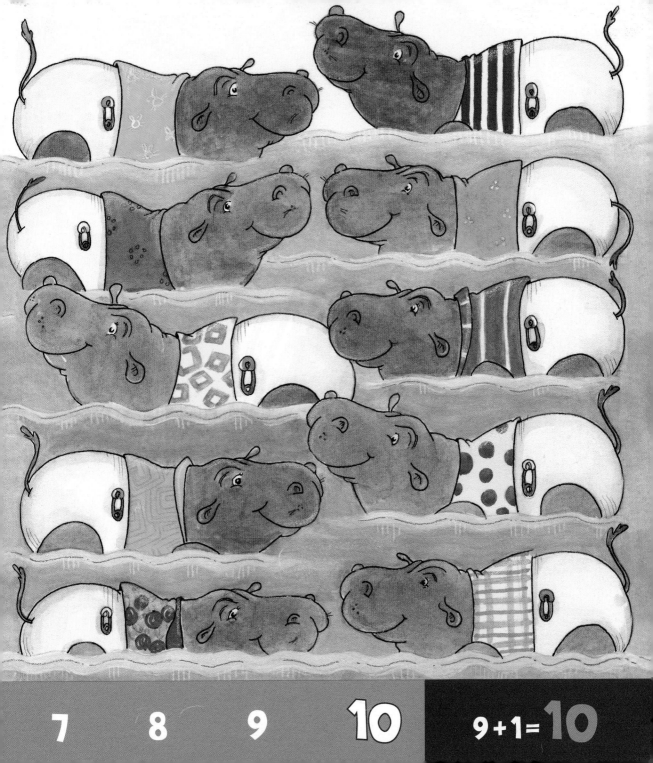

7 8 9 **10** 9+1= **10**

Words to Know

graze—to eat.

grunt—to make a short, low sound from the throat.

territory—an area belonging to a person or animal.

tusk—a large tooth that sticks out of the mouth.

twitch—to move with sudden motion.

Web Sites

To learn more about counting by from 1 to 10, visit ABDO Publishing Company on the World Wide Web at **www.abdopublishing.com**. Web sites about counting are featured on our Book Links page. These links are routinely monitored and updated to provide the most current information available.

1 2 3 4 5 6 7 8 9 10